Published by Creative Education
123 South Broad Street, Mankato, Minnesota 56001
Creative Education is an imprint of The Creative Company

Designed by Stephanie Blumenthal
Production design by Melinda Belter

Photographs by Richard Cummins, Frank Lambrecht, Kenneth Rapalee,
Eugene G. Schulz, Tom Till, and Ulrich Tutsch

Library of Congress Cataloging-in-Publication Data

Chapman, Lynne F. (Lynne Ferguson)
Medieval castles / by Lynne Ferguson Chapman.
p. cm. — (Designing the future)
Includes index
Summary: Describes the history, use, and structure of medieval castles.
ISBN 0-88682-687-X
1. Castles—Juvenile literature. 2. Castles—Europe—History—
Juvenile Literature. 3. Civilization, Medieval—Juvenile literature.
[1. Castles. 2. Civilization, Medieval.] I. Title. II. Series.
GT3550.C4   1999
944'.02—dc21   98-17174

9 8 7 6 5 4 3

DESIGNING THE FUTURE

MEDIEVAL CASTLES

LYNN FERGUSON CHAPMAN

CREATIVE EDUCATION

At least 3,000 years ago on the continent now known as Europe, primitive warriors wanted a place to live that would be out of reach of their enemies. They put up a rough shelter on high ground, then protected it by erecting banks and digging ditches around it. These Iron Age men had invented the first fortress, a sort of primitive castle. Since those days, castles have been built by civilizations all over the world but never more ambitiously than in Europe during the Middle Ages. In a period lasting approximately

Dunluce Castle, Northern Ireland

400 years, most of the world's biggest, strongest, and grandest castles were built. These amazing structures towered over a landscape that consisted mostly of small villages and farms. Today, most medieval castles remain as little more than crumbling ruins, but when they were newly built they must have been awe-inspiring, with colorful flags

Visitors to England's Dover Castle are exposed to thousands of years of history. The castle is built on the remains of a prehistoric hill-fort and also contains a Roman lighthouse and a Saxon church.

flapping from their towers and soldiers in bright armor patrolling their walls. Built, inhabited, and defended by the most powerful men of the era, these magnificent castles dominated the medieval world.

Living in a time of early exploration and wars

Kilkenny Castle, Ireland

Dunvegan Castle, Scotland

for domination, medieval kings and lords needed secure homes that could withstand attacks. Around 950, they began to build fortresses that we know as castles. The earliest castles in Europe were built in northern France by the Normans, who had settled there in the 10th century. Originally Vikings from Scandinavia, the warlike Normans were always looking for new conquests, and in 1066 their king, William, invaded England. The Normans won, and their ruler became King William I of England, best

Stirling Castle, Stirling, Scotland

known as William the Conqueror.

England's peasants must have suffered greatly during the next 20 years, as King William's lords demanded both hard labor and higher taxes to build about 100 castles. The Normans also introduced castle building to southern Italy, another of their strongholds. Sometime during the second half of the 11th century, the Norman ruler Robert Guiscard built a castle at Melfi. Thus began the great age of castle building. Strong walls and a moat made a castle easier to defend, but first the king or lord had to choose the site. A castle could be built in a large town, along a border, at a river crossing, or at the junction of two major roads. It had to be placed where it could best control the surrounding countryside.

Caerphilly Castle in South Wales, the earliest concentric castle in Britain and one of the largest castles in all of Europe, is situated in the middle of an artificial lake that was formed by damming a stream.

High ground offered defenders an advantage, so fortresses were often constructed at the tops of hills or on rocky cliffs. When a hill wasn't available, a builder could make his own; most of the earliest castles both in northern France and in England were built atop large artificial mounds of earth known as mottes. A high wooden fence enclosed the top of a motte, and inside this fence was a wooden tower. At the foot of the motte was another wooden fence, enclosing a courtyard

Veves Castle, Belgium

known as a bailey with a number of buildings for the lord's family and his followers. Castle residents spent most of their time in the bailey, but if attacked they could retreat to the tower on the motte. These castles were easy to build; nearly all 100 of the fortresses that William put up after seizing control of England were motte-and-bailey castles.

Enemies quickly discovered that the castles' wooden fences and towers were easy to burn or

Archer's window

O R I E N T A L

With their pagoda-like roofs and gables decorated to indicate the power of their owners, Japanese castles such as the one at Himeji were as beautiful as they were strong.

Gate to Henry II Keep, Dover Castle

lived in a city of modest wooden buildings, must have watched in amazement as this structure rose before them. As its centerpiece, the White Tower measured 115 feet (35 m) long and 90 feet (27 m) high.

Because a castle's entrance was its weakest point, the lord often constructed a gatehouse, with a group of towers, bridges, and barriers to protect it. Many gatehouses included a drawbridge which could be raised; a moat, designed to drown attackers who

knock down with battering rams. Some lords strengthened their castles with a stone wall known as a shell keep around the top of their motte. These castles were still vulnerable because of their numerous timber-framed buildings, so King William had his new castles constructed completely of stone. The most famous of these early fortifications was the Tower of London, built in 1078. Londoners, who

HARDWARE

Huge iron hinges were forged in order to hold the weight of the heavy doors that protected the inside of the castle.

Cawdor Castle, Scotland

tried to tunnel under the walls; and perhaps a barbican, an outer gatehouse. Building a stone castle was a huge, expensive under-taking. The largest ones would have cost millions of dollars by present-day stan-dards. They required hundreds of work-

Spotin Castle, Belgium

men and could take decades to finish. An architect or master mason directed the operation, assisted by many skilled craftsmen including masons, carpen-ters, and blacksmiths. But the men who did the back-breaking construction work were mostly out-of-work farmhands, pris-oners on parole, and others unwillingly forced into service. The only mechanical aids builders had were simple hoists, or cranes.

Despite the trouble and expense involved,

Würzburg Castle, Germany

North Solar Room, Buratty Castle, Ireland

castles were being built all over Europe by the 12th century. Building a castle usually assured a lord of greater power and prestige; unfortunately, the rapid spread of fortifications also guaranteed that many dark decades of struggle between powerful rulers lay ahead. While the Normans were busy building castles to secure their conquests in the late 11th and early 12th centuries, other European peoples were also experimenting with castle building and began to develop distinct regional styles.

The average Norman castle is sturdy and more or less square, but a typical castle in central Europe has a more long and narrow design; for example, the Swiss castle of Chillon, on an island in Lake Geneva, has a cigar-shaped layout. In Germany, Austria, and Czechoslovakia, high, pointed roofs are often found on castle turrets. The blending of architectural styles from western European and Islamic cultures resulted in distinctive castles in Spain. Elaborate brickwork and high battlements topped with small pyramids and decorated with fluting give the 15th-century Spanish castle of Coca a fanciful appearance.

Castle building in Europe took a great leap forward when westerners were exposed to a part of the world that was new to them. Between the 11th and 13th centuries European knights traveled several times

Arundel Castle, England

Pierre-Fronds Chateau, France

in Syria. Because this type of castle was equally strong at every point, it did not need to have a keep; instead, the various buildings within the central courtyard were protected by three lines of defense—a moat, outer walls, and higher inner walls. Every part of the defense protected or was protected by another part; for example, soldiers along the inner wall could fire over the heads of the outermost defenders. This type of fortress came to be known as a concentric castle.

to the Holy Land to try to free it from occupying Muslim armies. These knights, known as crusaders, were impressed by the Arab and Byzantine fortifications at places such as Constantinople and Antioch. When they won the First Crusade and established their own feudal states in the Middle East, they either rebuilt existing castles or constructed their own following the Arab model. The most famous of these crusader castles was the magnificent Krak des Chevaliers

Laarne Castle, Belgium

Raglan Castle, Wales

Returning crusaders began building concentric castles in Europe in the late 13th century. Perhaps the world's most perfect concentric castles were constructed in northern Wales by King Edward I of England, who needed to secure this volatile territory after defeating the scattered princes who had ruled there. Edward spared no expense in putting up eight of the most sophisticated castles ever built—including Caernarfon, Conway, and Harlech castles—in fewer than 10 years! Nearly 2,000 laborers worked on Caernarfon alone.

Primarily a castle was a fortress, but it was also a home to many people. The largest room in the castle, and the center of castle life, was the Great Hall. In early castles this was usually in the keep; later, the Great Hall was one of many stone buildings erected in the bailey. A Great Hall was usually at least 40 feet (12 m) long, but sometimes it was twice that

Bodian Castle, England

length. This vast room was where the castle dwellers gathered for their meals and sometimes enjoyed storytelling, music, and juggling. It was also where the lord held court to settle community disputes, and where he met with his steward, who organized day-to-day affairs. For many, the Great Hall was even a bedroom; unaccustomed to privacy, people simply laid straw mattresses in any available corner. Early halls were heated by open hearths rather than

Lichtenfels Castle, Germany

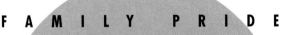

F A M I L Y   P R I D E

The crest over the entrance at Edinburg Castle, Scotland has the classic rampant lion on a gold shield.

Chillon Castle, Switzerland

Gravensteen Castle, Belgium

fireplaces, so rooms were probably smoky, foul-smelling, and cold.

The most comfortable room was the solar, the private chamber of the lord and lady. It often contained a curtained bed, the castle's best piece of furniture. Wall hangings helped to insulate and decorate the room. Along with guest rooms, the solar was often above the Great Hall on a second floor. In its bailey, a medieval castle included a whole range of buildings, including a kitchen and brewhouse, storage sheds, a barn and stables, a chapel, and a blacksmith's shop. A very large castle could have 100 servants—blacksmiths, horse groomers, falconers, cooks, bakers, brewers, gardeners, and laundresses.

Many castles housed permanent garrisons of

The Austrian castle of Hohensalzburg was begun in 1077 and its construction expanded for almost 600 years. Late medieval additions included beautiful red marble columns and paneled ceilings.

soldiers in the gatehouse. (The most common medieval fighting man was not a knight in armor but a foot soldier who fought with a lance or pike or who fired a bow.) Sometimes prisoners were also housed in the gatehouse. A prisoner of noble background might be held in a comfortable tower room for ransom, but most ordinary prisoners were tossed into the dungeon, a cold underground prison.

Dolbarden Castle, Wales

Chaplain's bedchamber, Bunratty Castle, Ireland

Castle walls often flared out at the base, allowing missiles dropped from above to bounce off toward the enemy and also making the walls harder to batter. Rounded towers offered protection against battering. Wide walkways along the tops of walls enabled defenders to move all the way around the castle quickly. Archers could hide behind the high sections on the battlements, known as merlons, and fire through the gaps between merlons, called crenels; for greater safety, they could shoot their arrows through the tall, narrow slits known as loops in the tower walls. The defenders also might erect hoardings, temporary wooden structures which overhung the walls; inside these, soldiers could remain protected while dropping missiles on their enemies through holes in the floor. In later castles hoardings were replaced by permanent stone structures called machicolations.

Thick walls and high towers were not a medieval castle's greatest strength. Only the most clever attacker could get past the numerous obstacles created for defense. The first was usually a moat. Many castles had a barbican, or outer gatehouse, to protect the bridge crossing the moat. Because a drawbridge could be raised, it offered further protection, as did a

O N   C E R E M O N Y

The throne rooms, where the reigning king or queen would conduct official business, were ornate and richly appointed.

Gallery, Ormond Castle, Ireland

portcullis. Even if attackers could get into the gatehouse, they had to watch out for murder holes, small openings in the roof through which defenders could shoot arrows, poke spears, drop stones, or perhaps even pour boiling water down on their enemies.

Azay-le-rideau, France

As castle defenses became stronger, attackers became more resourceful. They could scale the walls with ladders or hurl large stones or burning bundles over the castle walls using catapults or siege machines. With a huge, wooden siege tower filled with soldiers, they could release attackers into the castle. Or they could tunnel underneath, then erect wooden supports and set fire to them. Many sieges failed, however, and the castles that they targeted continued standing strong. As the Middle Ages waned, however, European society began to undergo dramatic changes. Soon the great castles, once nearly impenetrable, would become obsolete.

Gunpowder, introduced in Europe in the early

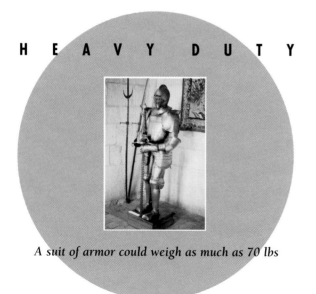

H E A V Y   D U T Y

A suit of armor could weigh as much as 70 lbs

Neuschwanstein Castle, Germany

14th century, was partly to blame for the ruination of the great castles. Cannons could easily knock down walls and rip through gates; defenders were almost helpless against it.

The decline of these castles was also due to social changes in Europe. The standard of Edward I's eight concentric castles was almost impossible to live up to. They were just too expensive, both to build and to garrison. By the 15th century, Europe was becoming more politically stable. Most lords preferred debating

Ruins of a castle

ideas in a drawing room to attacking each other's castles; wars became contests between armies on open battlefields. People also wanted more comfortable living conditions than a castle could offer, so they began to build manor houses with spacious rooms, glass windows, and fireplaces with chimneys.

Later generations of kings and nobles were inspired by the romance of the Middle Ages. King Henry VIII of England referred to the military forts he built in the 16th century as castles even though no one lived in them. In the 18th and 19th centuries, rulers and other wealthy men built lavish fairy tale-style castles, such as

Window seat in the great hall of Cahir Castle, Ireland

King Ludwig of Bavaria's Neuschwanstein Castle.

Today, only a few authentic medieval castles continue to be lived in. The most famous is Windsor Castle in England, the home of the Royal Family. Castles that have remained in private hands have become showplaces or luxury hotels for visitors.

With-out money from tourism, their owners could never afford to keep them up. These castles, with their elegant furnishings, formal gardens, exhibits, and gift

Stone Carving, Dublin, Ireland

Lismore Castle, Ireland

shops, no longer have much in common with the grim fortresses of the Middle Ages. Most medieval castles today are scenic ruins, usually maintained by governments or private trusts as historical landmarks. Many people delight in touring them, trying to picture the life that once went on within them. No other type of building stirs imaginations quite like the great medieval castles.

Beersel Castle, Belgium

31

I N D E X

B
bailey, 11, 19, 23
barbican, 14, 25

C
concentric castle, 9, 18, 19, 28
courtyard, 9
crenels, 24

D
Dover Castle, 6
drawbridge, 12, 25
dungeon, 23

F
First Crusade, 18
fortress(es), 5, 8, 9, 18, 31

G
gatehouse(s), 12, 14, 23, 25
Great Hall, 19

H
hoardings, 24

L
loops, 24

M
machicolations, 25
manor houses, 29
merlons, 24
Middle Ages, 5, 29, 31
moat, 9, 12, 25
motte(s), 9, 11, 12
murder holes, 26

N
Norman(s), 8, 9, 15

P
portcullis, 26

S
shell keep, 12
solar, 23

T
tower(s), 6, 11, 24, 25, 26

Neuschwanstein Castle in Germany